Pocketbooks – *available in both paperback and digital formats*

360 Degree Feedback*
Absence Management
Appraisals
Assertiveness
Balance Sheet
Body Language
Business Planning
Career Transition
Coaching
Cognitive Behavioural Coaching
Communicator's
Competencies
Confidence
Creative Manager's
C.R.M.
Cross-cultural Business
Customer Service
Decision-making
Delegation
Developing People
Discipline & Grievance
Diversity*
Emotional Intelligence
Empowerment*
Energy and Well-being
Facilitator's
Feedback
Flexible Working*

Handling Complaints
Handling Resistance
Icebreakers
Impact & Presence
Improving Efficiency
Improving Profitability
Induction
Influencing
Interviewer's
I.T. Trainer's
Key Account Manager's
Leadership
Learner's
Management Models
Manager's
Managing Assessment Centres
Managing Budgets
Managing Cashflow
Managing Change
Managing Customer Service
Managing Difficult Participants
Managing Recruitment
Managing Upwards
Managing Your Appraisal
Marketing
Mediation
Meetings
Memory

Mentoring
Motivation
Negotiator's
Networking
NLP
Nurturing In
Openers &
People Man
Performance Management
Personal Success
Positive Mental Attitude
Presentations
Problem Behaviour
Project Management
Psychometric Testing
Resolving Conflict
Reward*
Sales Excellence
Salesperson's*
Self-managed Development
Starting In Management
Storytelling
Strategy
Stress
Succeeding at Interviews
Sustainability
Tackling Difficult Conversations
Talent Management

Training Needs Analysis
Transfer of Learning
Virtual Teams
Vocal Skills
Working Relationships
Workplace Politics
Writing Skills

* only available as an e-book

Pocketfiles

Trainer's Blue Pocketfile of
Ready-to-use Activities

Trainer's Green Pocketfile of
Ready-to-use Activities

Trainer's Red Pocketfile of
Ready-to-use Activities

To order please visit us at **www.pocketbook.co.uk**

05.08.14

ORDER FORM

Your details

Name _____

Position _____

Company _____

Address _____

_____

_____

Telephone _____

Fax _____

E-mail _____

VAT No. (EC companies) _____

Your Order Ref _____

Please send me:

		No. copies
The Cross-cultural Business	Pocketbook	[ ]
The _____	Pocketbook	[ ]
The _____	Pocketbook	[ ]
The _____	Pocketbook	[ ]

Order by Post
MANAGEMENT
POCKETBOOKS LTD
LAUREL HOUSE, STATION APPROACH,
ALRESFORD, HAMPSHIRE SO24 9JH UK

Order by Phone, Fax or Internet
Telephone: +44 (0)1962 735573
Facsimile: +44 (0)1962 733637
E-mail: sales@pocketbook.co.uk
Web: www.pocketbook.co.uk

Customers in USA should contact:
Management Pocketbooks
2427 Bond Street, University Park, IL 60466
Telephone: 866 620 6944   Facsimile: 708 534 7803
E-mail: mp.orders@ware-pak.com
Web: www.managementpocketbooks.com

THE
CROSS-CULTURAL BUSINESS
POCKETBOOK

By John Mattock
Drawings by Phil Hailstone

"On our business development courses, we emphasise cultural sensitivity, because we know it pays off! This pocketbook is a good starting point."
Evy Claesson, Ericsson Radio Systems AB

"A real understanding of cross-cultural issues has proved invaluable, both for developing our own global network, and for serving clients operating around the world."
Chris Sermon, PricewaterhouseCoopers

"Leaders in our company face many complex issues, including cultural diversity. This book offers a practical approach."
Sven Gatenheim, SCA Hygiene Products

Published by:
Management Pocketbooks Ltd
Laurel House, Station Approach, Alresford, Hants SO24 9JH, U.K.
Tel: +44 (0)1962 735573   Fax: +44 (0)1962 733637
E-mail: sales@pocketbook.co.uk
Website: www.pocketbook.co.uk

All rights reserved. No part of this publication may be reproduced, stored in a retrieval system
or transmitted in any form, or by any means, electronic, mechanical, photocopying, recording
or otherwise, without the prior permission of the publishers.

This edition published 1999. Reprinted 2001, 2004, 2006, 2008, 2014.

©   John Mattock 1999.

British Library Cataloguing-in-Publication Data – A catalogue record for this book is available
from the British Library.

ISBN 978 1 870471 73 2

Design, typesetting and graphics by **efex ltd**.   Printed in U.K.

WHO SHOULD READ THIS BOOK?

This book is for managers who have an international dimension to their work. It offers stimulating perspectives on how 'foreigners' behave, and how they see you as a 'foreigner'. There are many practical tips on how to improve communication across the culture gap, how to avoid unnecessary culture shock and, generally, how to play the culture game and enjoy it!

You will get something out of it if you:

- Travel abroad on business
- Act as host on your home territory to foreign business partners
- Communicate from headquarters to foreign subsidiaries, or vice-versa
- Work on projects as part of a multinational team
- Organise conferences where the nationalities will be mixed
- Develop the careers of staff who must travel
- Want to improve your relationship with a business contact overseas
- Feel curious about other ways of seeing the world, other ways of doing business

CONTENTS

WHY CULTURE COUNTS

WHY CULTURE COUNTS

THE WORLD HAS SHRUNK

Corporations have moved on, from 'international' to 'multinational' to 'global'. Markets cross national and continental boundaries; products and services, specifications and brands, contracts and campaigns - all are conceived for worldwide use.

Commonplace technical miracles bring people together as never before: mobiles, laptops with modems, the internet ... many take the technology for granted. Perhaps we become complacent or lazy about our way of communicating at the human level?

The skies are full of managers and professionals:

- Travelling to do business with foreign customers, suppliers and investors

- Attending international conferences – in-company or pan-occupational

- Reporting to headquarters or visiting local branches overseas

- Relocating career and family to far-flung parts of the world

EMPATHY IS GOOD BUSINESS

Imagine a choice between two foreign suppliers offering similar price and quality, and terms and conditions.

- One displays curiosity about your country - its people, history, economy, institutions, art and language - and seems keen to build good working relationships according to your local habits

- The other doesn't bother: this organisation sticks to the business in hand, and expects all business partners to fit in with the 'normal' or 'correct' way of seeing and doing things

Which one will you choose to do business with? Which will you recommend to your network of contacts? Which will you seek to emulate the next time **you** do business abroad?

CULTURE INFLUENCES PERCEPTIONS

The way you see the world is directly influenced by your background: your parents brought you up, your teachers educated you, and your friends conditioned you *according to the tacit rules of your local culture.*

Your views on right and wrong, duty and pleasure, order and chaos, reason and emotion, pride and shame - are coloured by the filters of culture.

As a manager, you need successful interaction with others: sharing ideas, anticipating their needs, and helping them improve performance. If they see the world through the same filters as you, that's fine. But if they have different ... *foreign* ... *ALIEN* perceptions and attitudes, then you have a trickier job to do.

> *'If I want to succeed in guiding a human being ... I must find him where he is ... to help a person, I must of course understand more than he does, but above all I must understand what he understands.'*
> **Kierkegaard**

CULTURE AFFECTS BEHAVIOUR

Racial prejudice is a bad thing:

> *'Any of those people
> is intrinsically inferior to any of these people,
> and so has fewer human rights.'*

To dump a national stereotype on an individual person is destructive:

> *'She's late again; typical!'*

> *'He's good on the detail, but a creative zero.
> What can you expect?'*

> *'He's busy covering his back - they all do!'*

Yet, you can predict with some accuracy how a person from a given culture is *likely* to behave. And if you plan *without* taking culture into account, your project will be under threat.

(5)

CASE EXAMPLE 1

The Swiss chief executive addressed a conference of managers from various national subsidiaries, describing his ideas for the future. Comments in the bar that evening:

> 'For me there was too much pie-in-the-sky. Thirty minutes he talked, and we got practically no concrete facts.' **The German**

> 'I'm concerned that he seems to know so little about our local client base ... the way they really are. We have so many small customers who don't fit the statistical projections.' **The Italian**

> 'Well, if that's his view of the future, I'm outa here. No drive, no determination, no leadership, no vision.' **The American**

> 'I don't know why you're all taking it so seriously. Surely you were expecting that sort of twaddle, weren't you? I propose to ignore it and carry on as normal.' **The Briton**

WHY CULTURE COUNTS

CASE EXAMPLE 2

The English manager was frustrated: he was getting on well with his Hungarian staff but now they had suddenly turned unco-operative.

He had taken the 40 of them away for a teambuilding weekend. There was a great party on Friday night and all seemed very positive. At noon on Saturday he announced: "Thanks for working so hard this morning. Now we'll break a little early for lunch, so you can enjoy the sunshine. BUT PLEASE, come back prompt at 2 o'clock. If you are late, you will miss the start of an important and entertaining exercise. So 2 o'clock PLEASE. Jó étvágyat!"

At 2 o'clock there were half-a-dozen Hungarians assembled, staring at their shoes or smoking in the corridor. Another five or six trickled in over the next half-hour. It was all rather embarrassing.

He turned to his Hungarian deputy: "What did I do wrong?"

"Although you don't realise it, you gave them a choice: either to arrive on time and prove nothing, or to be late and demonstrate that we are a free people now!"

This was one year after the Soviet withdrawal.

DEVELOP A STRATEGY

If you are convinced of the importance of cross-cultural issues, then develop a strategy for dealing with them.

Code of Cross-cultural Conduct

1. We appreciate and enjoy cultural diversity

2. We accept that our own perceptions are coloured by our upbringing, within our native culture

3. We try to empathise with the other's view, knowing that it will be influenced by his or her background

4. We do some homework to understand that background better

5. We are open-minded; we do not dump a national stereotype on an individual

WHY CULTURE COUNTS

EXERCISE: ASSIGNMENT IN RUBOVIA

You are on your first trip to Rubovia. In your briefcase is a wad of information about the business aspects of your visit, to read on the plane.

As you board the Air Rubov flight, you notice that the chap just in front of you is greeted by the crew as a familiar face - in a language you have never heard before (Rubovian, presumably).

Now you find yourself sitting beside him, and he wishes you good afternoon in excellent English.

Over the next couple of hours, you have a wonderful opportunity to benefit from a free 'seminar' on Rubovian business culture. (Most people are very happy to talk about their national way of life.)

What sort of subjects will you try to explore? (Our answer is on the next page.)

ASSIGNMENT IN RUBOVIA: OUR ANSWER

These are the sort of questions you might ask your Rubovian informant (not in any order of priority):

- How do you say 'Hello'/'Thank you'/'Cheers!' in Rubovian?
- What's the local style of handshakes/hugs/kisses?
- Is it expected to offer gifts? What is appropriate?
- What's best to eat and drink?
- Are there any religious taboos I should know about?
- Do Rubovians attach importance to personal relationships when they do business?
- Do they worry about deadlines and punctuality, or are they relaxed about such things?
- Do they admire quick, bold decisions or do they favour a cautious approach?
- Is documentation important in business life, or is it 'My word is my bond'?
- What do Rubovians find amusing in my national culture (if they know about it)?
- What's everybody in Rubovia talking about at the moment?

MODELLING A CULTURE

MODELS, GURUS ... AND A SCORESHEET

This section covers **generic** cross-cultural issues: ideas that apply to any situation where any two cultures meet. (Later there are some pages of **culture-specific** material - notes on a handful of cultural groupings.)

Key ideas in generic cross-cultural studies - be they training courses, popular books or learned articles - are often called 'models'. A model is a way of putting shape on the world - imposing order and making sense of it.

Important models have been developed by 'gurus' in the cross-cultural world. We have taken key aspects of the gurus' models, and combined them into one diagnostic 'toolkit' - the scoresheet on pages 26-43.

WHY BUILD A MODEL?

I have already spoken against racial stereotyping. But what to replace it with? Once you accept that national or regional origins might influence people's perception and behaviour, you need a way to sort the information out.

The study of anthropology used to be pretty straightforward. Armed with pencil and paper, and perhaps a Kodak, the anthropologist spent a couple of years observing tribal behaviour in, say, Tuvalu, and then wrote a best-selling book called 'Getting Married in Tuvalu'. The book fairly simply described people and events.

After WWII, *structuralism* emerged. Frenchman Claude Lévi-Strauss built a huge reputation by observing and deducing hidden currents beneath a variety of cultures.

'... individual phenomena can be understood only in relationship to other elements in the same system ... using a limited set of contrasts or oppositions.' **Cambridge Encyclopaedia**

We return to the idea of *contrasts* and *oppositions* later. Back to our basic lesson in model building ...

(13)

LEARNING BY OBSERVATION

Look at the world, see something interesting or new, ask a few questions, and listen carefully to the answers. Then think about the answers you have received and try to make a few connections and predictions: 'So that means...'

Then have another look at what's going on.

We do this as children quite naturally. This is how we build a model of the world around us.

As adults, this is the best way for us to approach another culture.

THE LEARNING LOOP

OBSERVE
AN EVENT OR BEHAVIOUR
'Look what they just did!'

REFLECT
ON THE MOTIVATION
'What might make them do that?'

INVESTIGATE
LOCAL BACKGROUND
'Any explanations for this attitude?'

ENRICH
YOUR EXPLANATORY MODEL
'How does this fit the big picture?'

MODELLING A CULTURE

CASE EXAMPLE 3

Jeanne was touring her company's national subsidiaries. She spent several days in Tokyo and, as she was leaving, the boss gave her a gift. It was so beautifully wrapped, it seemed a pity to open it. When she did, she found a small souvenir with the company logo on it - quite probably less valuable than the ornate packaging.

Observation: Packaging is more important than the gift.

Reflection: Is this about keeping up appearances? Ceremonial? The value of paper?

Investigation: Japan's fertile land is very crowded - cities, rice paddies, fish farms. No room for trees.

Enrichment: If paper is rare and precious, this throws light on the ritual importance of business cards.

Jeanne's next few days were spent in Moscow. Once again, there was a gift - a pretty lacquer box with a firebird design but not wrapped at all! Hmmm ... plenty of timber in Russia.

MAKING OBSERVATIONS

Airport: Are people queuing or barging? Shaking hands, embracing or keeping their distance? Stylish exhibitionists or shy and unassuming? Is their speech monotonous or *coloratura?*

Taxi: Look at how people drive and watch how your driver reacts. Note the architecture: what period dominates? Purely native or old colonial influences?

Hotel: Watch the local TV stations – what music, what comedy, sophisticated advertising? Dinner time – sybaritic or functional? Flow of conversation - monologues interspersed with silences, or a chaotic cacophony?

Meeting: How does the hierarchy work? How are decisions made? Are agendas adhered to? Are explanations detailed? Do people make jokes? Over lunch, do people talk only shop, or TV/sport/politics/family?

CHANNELS FOR REFLECTION

You see an example of *rebelliousness* or *conformism, material ambition* or *spiritual awareness, individual risk-taking* or *communal risk-avoidance, impatience* or *self-control:* where does it come from?

When I started working internationally, I tried to clear my mind of prejudice. The French were not pompous, nor the Swedes dull, nor the Chinese aggressive. Over the years I have found a factual basis for these distorted images; there is no smoke without fire.

- French society does set great store by status and position; self-effacement is seldom seen, rarely admired.

- Swedes call *themselves* dull. Children are taught: 'Don't go thinking you're anybody special!'.

- Talk in Shanghai is not polite by our standards: 'What you want?' 'You got it wrong!' 'Hurry up'.

Pompous ... dull ... aggressive. These are damaging prejudices because they express negative characteristics. But what about *status-conscious ... steady ... direct* instead?

AREAS FOR INVESTIGATION

Your job as a model-builder is not to prove cause-and-effect. Nobody can say for sure: 'The people of this culture behave in such a way *because*...' Life is not so simple; a culture is a very complex system.

However, within a complex system, there are nodes of influence. When you are looking for 'explanations for an attitude', you will often be able to say: 'It surely must have something to do with...'

POPULATION DENSITY   **ECONOMIC HISTORY**   **COMMUNICATIONS**

FAMILY/TRIBAL STRUCTURE

PHYSICAL GEOGRAPHY   *LANGUAGE*   **RELIGION**

MIGRATION   **CLIMATE**

(19)

MODELLING A CULTURE

RUBOVIAN INVESTIGATIONS

You survive your first quick visit to Rubovia, and it looks as if you might be committed to a longer project. You decide to enrich your model with some further research.

Of course, if you are a big reader, you can go for the official 'Ten-Volume History of Rubovia', and get swamped with detail. (But if you're that type, why are you reading a Management Pocketbook?) Much better is 'The Children's Illustrated Encyclopaedia Rubovica'. The information will be digestible, and probably include everything the average Rubovian knows about the country's past.

Search under 'Rubovia' at your favourite Internet bookstore. Phone the Rubovian embassy or Chamber of Commerce and ask for an information pack. Browse news-stand publications when you land.

Best of all, find a compatriot of yours who has lived and worked in Rubovia, and offer lunch. Then kick off the conversation with the simple question: 'What mistakes did you make in your first year in Rubovia?'.

MEET THE GURUS (1)

Following the structuralist idea (see page 13), social scientists have studied the cultures of business.

Edward Hall: This American studied the corporate cultures of Europe and identified two key polarities:

- 'High Context' (where communication is subtle and oblique, eg: France) versus 'Low Context' (where matters are spelt out in detail, eg: Sweden)

- 'Monochronic' (where things happen in strict sequence, eg: Germany) versus 'Polychronic' (where timetables and priorities are endlessly juggled, eg: Italy)

Low Context/Monochronic cultures in N.W. Europe are task-focused: you are valued for the work you do. High Context/ Polychronic cultures to the South East focus on people: get on well with the people, and all runs smoothly.

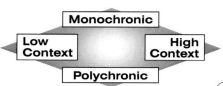

MODELLING A CULTURE

MEET THE GURUS (2)

Geert Hofstede: Dutch. Added new polarities to the system:

- 'High Power-Distance' cultures encourage superiors to exert power (India). 'Low Power-Distance' societies compel bosses to listen to subordinates (Israel).

- 'High Uncertainty-Avoidance' cultures eschew risks (Japan). 'Low Uncertainty-Avoidance' cultures admire risk-takers (Denmark).

- 'Individualist' cultures value initiative (Britain). 'Collectivist' cultures demand loyalty to the clan (Iran).

- 'Masculine' cultures stress ambition and prowess (Australia). 'Feminine' cultures favour ecology and justice (Netherlands).

Terence Brake: American. Defined the requirements of 'the global leader'. What skills must be developed to meet the transnational business challenge?

John Mole: English. Grouped the EC states on a scale 'organic *versus* systematic organisation'. Mediterraneans come out organic and Northerners systematic. The other dimension is 'individual *versus* group leadership': Spain and France favour strong leadership, while UK, Denmark and the Netherlands prefer teamwork.

MEET THE GURUS (3)

Fons Trompenaars: Dutch. Worldwide, he analysed responses to ethical puzzle questions:

- Would you bend the truth to protect a friend from the law? (Canadians NO, South Koreans YES)

- Should the team take responsibility for one member's mistake? (Russia NO, Indonesia YES)

- If you are upset at work, should you show your feelings? (Japan NO, Italy YES)

- Should you do a personal favour for your boss? (Australia NO, China YES)

- Do family links and the right school affect your view of other people? (Denmark NO, East Germany YES)

Richard D Lewis: English. One grand polarity: 'Linear-active' (eg: N.W. Europeans, Americans) versus 'Multi-active' (eg: Latins, Arabs, Indians). A third dimension: 'Reactive' cultures which prioritise courtesy, respect, and calm response (eg: Asians, Finns).

Nothing really new for twenty years now; none of the world's business cultures is about to spring a big surprise.

SCORESHEET

I have taken all the contrasts, opposites, polarities and scales I could find (18 in all) and grouped them together in three main areas, six polarities to each area:

Perception & Cognition

How does a member of a given culture see the world, interpret events, think things through?

Self & Society

What is the view on rights and duties in the given culture? How are people socialised?

Decisions & Communication

How is power used in organisations? How is information handled? How are messages spread?

MODELLING A CULTURE

HOW TO USE THE SCORESHEET

1. Recognise that it's all relative

If we say that the Zürich Swiss are punctual by habit, we don't mean they are never late: that would be an unrealistic absolute. We can say, however, that they are punctual by comparison with, say, the Dublin Irish. (Proverb: 'When the good Lord created time, he created plenty.')

2. Start with your own culture

For each polarity, score your own culture by circling one number on the scale. Try this exercise with a small group of compatriots, setting the question: 'How does the rest of the world see us?' or 'How likely is one to encounter this attitude in our home culture: how 'typical' is it?'.

3. Focus on your target culture

Now score the foreign culture you are working with, in a different colour! If there are gaps in your knowledge, fill them (see page 20). Look for major deviations - two points or more - between your own culture and the target.

PERCEPTION & COGNITION (1)

DECISIVE	**SUBMISSIVE**
We control our lives, make free choices, anticipate consequences	Our destinies are dictated by our god(s), fate or environment

1	2	3	4	5	6

Observations _____

_____

_____

PERCEPTION & COGNITION (2)

THEORETICAL
Ideas are more useful within an orthodox conceptual framework

PRAGMATIC
It's OK to meet phenomena case by case, learning by experience

1	2	3	4	5	6

Observations _____

_____

_____

PERCEPTION & COGNITION (3)

UNIVERSAL
Some ideas/concepts are absolute, and can be applied in all situations

CIRCUMSTANTIAL
Theories are interpreted in line with common sense/human need

1	2	3	4	5	6

Observations _____

_____

_____

PERCEPTION & COGNITION (4)

LOOSE TIME

Deadlines are only guidelines: 'They won't mind waiting a bit longer'

TIGHT TIME

Delay equals failure: 'This project must run on schedule or else...'

1   *2*   *3*   *4*   *5*   *6*

Observations _____

_____

_____

PERCEPTION & COGNITION (5)

MULTIPLE EVENT

Clever people handle several ideas at once: the art of juggling

SINGLE EVENT

One at a time to avoid confusion: interruptions/ distractions are bad

| 1 | 2 | 3 | 4 | 5 | 6 |

Observations _____

_____

_____

PERCEPTION & COGNITION (6)

QUICK RESULTS	BIG PICTURE
Mechanistic/impatient; actions now should bring satisfaction soon	Holistic/patient; we think and act in the broad context of past and future

| 1 | 2 | 3 | 4 | 5 | 6 |

Observations _____

_____

_____

MODELLING A CULTURE

SELF & SOCIETY (1)

OUTGOING/INFORMAL

Our circle of acquaintance is wide and flexible; we do not harbour secrets

PRIVATE/RESERVED

We share our inner thoughts only with close friends and family

1	2	3	4	5	6

Observations _____

_____

_____

32

SELF & SOCIETY (2)

PERSONAL FULFILMENT

Encouragement and reward for individual talent and initiative

LOYALTY TO THE TRIBE

Duties are fixed by tradition, autocratic leaders or team needs

1	2	3	4	5	6

Observations _____

_____

_____

SELF & SOCIETY (3)

PRESCRIPTIVE	**FLEXIBLE**
Rules of conduct must not be bent; society suffers if they are	Sometimes we can ignore laws; respect your conscience and friends

Observations _____

_____

_____

SELF & SOCIETY (4)

DOING & MEASURING
High status goes with performance and achievement

BEING & FEELING
Living life well is the greatest accomplishment; work is only part of it

1	2	3	4	5	6

Observations _____

_____

_____

SELF & SOCIETY (5)

RELATIONSHIP					TASK
'If we can get on well, the work will be pleasant and fruitful'					'If we can do a good job together, we might get closer as people'

| 1 | 2 | 3 | 4 | 5 | 6 |

Observations _____

_____

_____

SELF & SOCIETY (6)

CO-OPERATION/CONSENSUS

Decisions by group synergy can be smoothly implemented

COMPETITION/CONFLICT

Forceful advocacy defeats opposition and brings success

1	2	3	4	5	6

Observations _____

_____

_____

DECISIONS & COMMUNICATION (1)

SUGGESTION

'I'm sure you'll get the gist of my idea without tedious over-explanation'

STATEMENT

'We'll both be more comfortable if I spell this out to avoid ambiguity'

1	2	3	4	5	6

Observations _____

_____

_____

DECISIONS & COMMUNICATION (2)

CONTEXTUAL
Plenty of background information helps us to understand things better

DIRECT
We move directly to the proposal, handling context questions later

| 1 | 2 | 3 | 4 | 5 | 6 |

Observations _____

_____

_____

DECISIONS & COMMUNICATION (3)

EMOTIONAL

Few inhibitions about expressing joy, anger, fear, passion, regret ...

CONTAINED

Embarrassment and friction can come from displays of emotion

| 1 | 2 | 3 | 4 | 5 | 6 |

Observations _____

_____

_____

DECISIONS & COMMUNICATION (4)

AVOIDING RISK

Beware precedents/
consequences; Look Before
You Leap

EMBRACING RISK

Seize every opportunity
without dithering; Who
Dares Wins

| 1 | 2 | 3 | 4 | 5 | 6 |

Observations _____

_____

_____

DECISIONS & COMMUNICATION (5)

	HIERARCHICAL				DEMOCRATIC	
	Good organisation requires clear direction from above				Power is distributed; everybody contributes to decisions	
1	2	3	4	5	6

Observations _____

_____

_____

DECISIONS & COMMUNICATION (6)

MERIT	STANDING
Respect is given to those who have earned it - including leaders	Respect goes to those with the right age/class/ qualifications

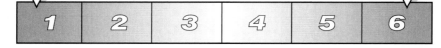

Observations _____

_____

_____

SUMMARY: THE 18 POLARITIES

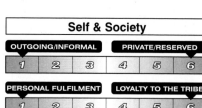

Perception & Cognition

DECISIVE			SUBMISSIVE		
1	2	3	4	5	6

THEORETICAL			PRAGMATIC		
1	2	3	4	5	6

UNIVERSAL			CIRCUMSTANTIAL		
1	2	3	4	5	6

LOOSE TIME			TIGHT TIME		
1	2	3	4	5	6

MULTIPLE EVENT			SINGLE EVENT		
1	2	3	4	5	6

QUICK RESULTS			BIG PICTURE		
1	2	3	4	5	6

Self & Society

OUTGOING/INFORMAL			PRIVATE/RESERVED		
1	2	3	4	5	6

PERSONAL FULFILMENT			LOYALTY TO THE TRIBE		
1	2	3	4	5	6

PRESCRIPTIVE			FLEXIBLE		
1	2	3	4	5	6

SUMMARY: THE 18 POLARITIES

DOING & MEASURING			BEING & FEELING		
1	2	3	4	5	6

RELATIONSHIP			TASK		
1	2	3	4	5	6

CO-OPERATION/CONSENSUS			COMPETITION/CONFLICT		
1	2	3	4	5	6

Decisions & Communication

SUGGESTION			STATEMENT		
1	2	3	4	5	6

CONTEXTUAL			DIRECT		
1	2	3	4	5	6

EMOTIONAL			CONTAINED		
1	2	3	4	5	6

AVOIDING RISK			EMBRACING RISK		
1	2	3	4	5	6

HIERARCHICAL			DEMOCRATIC		
1	2	3	4	5	6

MERIT			STANDING		
1	2	3	4	5	6

45

CASE EXAMPLE 4

APPLYING THE TOOL

Claes Persson worked for a small software design company, staffed by like-minded individuals from the same university town in central Sweden.

A tactical merger was taking place with a company based in Rubovia and Claes and his colleagues agreed to spend a little time on the culture issue. Claes was especially motivated, as he was off on a 2-year secondment, with his family, in the Rubovian capital.

As Step 1 they had a coffee-and-cake session to discuss their feelings about working with Rubovians: what advantages might it bring, what frictions might there be?

Step 2 was the 18-polarity grid (pages 26-43). Claes asked the management team to complete the scoring in a one-hour discussion on the question: *'AS SWEDES IN OUR HOME MARKET, WHAT IS OUR WORKING CULTURE?'*

Claes took all the scores of 1 or 6, and called them 'Primary Characteristics'; 2s or 5s were 'Secondary Traits'. The results are listed opposite. 3s and 4s were ignored as 'neutral and uninteresting'!

CASE EXAMPLE 4

HOW CLAES'S HOME CULTURE SCORED

PRIMARY CHARACTERISTICS	• TIGHT TIME
	• PRIVATE/RESERVED
	• DEMOCRATIC
SECONDARY TRAITS	• DECISIVE
	• CIRCUMSTANTIAL
	• PRESCRIPTIVE
	• TASK
	• CO-OPERATION/CONSENSUS
	• AVOIDING RISK
	• MERIT

CASE EXAMPLE 4

CLAES'S TARGET CULTURE

Through the Trade Council and Chamber of Commerce, Claes got in touch with local business people who had experience of Rubovia, and pumped them for their observations. He read a book, watched a video, surfed the net and visited a Rubovian delicatessen. He started to fill in a scoresheet.

A small delegation of his new Rubovian colleagues paid a visit to Sweden, and Claes volunteered to host them. He watched and listened closely as they asked questions about the Swedes' organisation and people's way of life. Over two lunches and a celebratory dinner, at which he sat beside the commercial attaché from the Rubovian embassy, he filled in some of the missing detail.

CASE EXAMPLE 4

CLAES'S CONCLUSIONS

Perception & Cognition

SCORING: Visitors scored a 1 on **UNIVERSAL**, against the Swedes' 5 on **CIRCUMSTANTIAL**. The Rubovians preferred rules to guidelines.

MEANING: Could be trouble: the Swedish software designers ran well on a loose rein; were the software factories in Rubovia more disciplined?

Self & Society

SCORING: A big gap here between **OUTGOING/INFORMAL** and **PRIVATE/RESERVED:** Rubovians thrive on intimate conversations about private matters.

MEANING: Little danger: Claes's stiffer Swedish colleagues experienced slight discomfort, but most enjoyed loosening up a bit.

Decisions & Communication

SCORING: Rubovians score high on **STANDING** - unlike their hosts' strong **MERIT** scoring.

MEANING: Be on best behaviour in the company of high-rank Rubovians.

CODE OF CONDUCT

On page 8, we gave you the first few rules for successful cross-cultural dealings. Here is the next batch:

Code of Cross-cultural Conduct

6. Once trust is established with our foreign partner, we openly discuss how our different cultural backgrounds might be affecting the issue.

7. We begin with a formal, polite manner, and await signals of informality from our partner.

8. We remain true to ourselves, resisting the temptation to mimic our partner's mannerisms

COMMUNICATION
ACROSS CULTURES

COMMUNICATION ACROSS CULTURES

WHY IT'S TOUGH

The words we speak constitute only a small part of our communication. The way we look and move, our tone of voice, the assumed context of what we are saying - all these carry more of the message than the nouns, verbs and adjectives we compile into sentences.

So, we are 'more comfortable with our own kind', where we can easily read and understand body language, non-verbal signals, and the sub-text of humour/despair/irony. We are confident that other people are receiving **our** messages loud and clear. Communication within our own cultures is second nature.

An exercise in culture shock

- Take up your pen and sign your name on a sheet of paper. Now do it again another five times. That's comfortable and easy.

- Now hold the pen in your 'wrong' hand and sign your name again. Clumsy? Stressful? Does the signature really look like yours?

That's what it's like working - and especially communicating - in a foreign culture!

COMMUNICATION ACROSS CULTURES

FRAMEWORK

In this section, we tackle the questions of:

 How to be clear   **How to be convincing**   **How to make the right impression**

These are key considerations when we are talking to a local customer, supplier or investor, in our common native language, on familiar subjects. Are the rules different when that business partner is in another country or on another continent? Certainly.

- Sometimes the rules are **reinforced**. For example, when you make a presentation, it is important to pause from time to time to let your message sink in. When you are speaking in English to a group of Venezuelans, *pause more often and for longer!*

- Sometimes the rules are **changed**. In Scandinavia, lots of smiling can indicate insincerity; in Japan it can be a sign of social embarrassment; in Russia it might suggest that you are a bit dim-witted.

HOW TO BE CLEAR (1)

English is the language of international business, the result of a complex historical accident. At conference table, on dockside and over video-link, English is used - *even if there is no native English-speaker present.*

> *'The English language does not belong to the British, you know'*
> **Turkish import-export trader**

There is nothing intrinsically superior about English. Its rich vocabulary makes for great poetry, but for negotiating a deal or hammering out a strategy, Esperanto would do just as well. There is now a new 'global English': less refined but more effective for cross-cultural communication.

COMMUNICATION ACROSS CULTURES

HOW TO BE CLEAR (2)

GRADE YOUR LANGUAGE

Our advice on 'global English' is chiefly directed to readers whose first language is English (and, perhaps, those North West Europeans whose English is so good it no longer feels like a foreign language).

Quite probably you studied a foreign language at school, and gave it up at the age of 16 or 18. How well could you use it now? Could you handle a sales negotiation in French, or run a training seminar in German?

Always remember, the foreign business partner who works with you in English has invested years of study and practice. Respect that fact, and respect the limitations he or she faces.

At the first meeting, listen to the quality of the person's English: smooth and rapid? Wide vocabulary and clever use of idiom? In this case, you just have to speak clearly and avoid crazy colloquialisms ('It's a no-brainer'; 'Odds-on he'll say no'; 'She's winding you up'). Long pauses? Frequent grammar mistakes? Clumsy idioms? In this case you need to make some concessions.

HOW TO BE CLEAR (3)

SLOW DOWN

This...does...not...mean...you...should...pause...after...each...word...and...speak...in...a... machine-like...monotone...with...each...syll-ab-le...dis-tinct-ly...pro-nounced.

This is known as the 'watch my lips' syndrome, and it appears very patronising: "I am speaking to you like this because I don't think you're very bright".

The right way to do it...is to recognise that people listen...to little clumps of words...and then need a little time...to sort out what the words mean.

Of course, this is the purpose of full stops, commas, colons and such like on the printed page: they help us to break the text up in our minds into something resembling the natural breath groups of human speech.

We have all met English speakers who gabble, and know how agonising it can be to listen to them for a long time. For a foreigner listening to English as a foreign language, the pain threshold is much lower.

HOW TO BE CLEAR (4)

PUT PLENTY OF COLOUR IN YOUR VOICE

...and you HELP them to *understand*...by getting **loud**er...on the *KEY WORDS*...

ensuring your voice **rises** and **falls** according to the meaning of the phrase.

Of all the European languages, English is the one where the music (emphasis, intonation) of the words gives most clue to their meaning.

57

HOW TO BE CLEAR (5)

EXERCISE: TEMPO & INTONATION

Imagine you are to speak the text below to a group of non-native speakers. Mark with a // the points where you will pause, with a _____ the syllables you will emphasise, and with little arrows ↗ ↘, the places where your voice will rise and fall. Then read it out loud, ideally recording your voice for critical playback later.

good afternoon everybody I'm glad to see so many familiar faces here today and I'm looking forward to making some new friends this evening over dinner now before I hand over to Paco to outline today's working agenda I'd like to spend a few minutes explaining how each of you can contribute to the meeting and how each of you can get the most benefit from the proceedings does that seem like a good idea

COMMUNICATION ACROSS CULTURES

HOW TO BE CLEAR (6)

TRIANGULATE YOUR MAIN IDEAS

Or, to put it more simply, say everything three times in slightly different ways, giving your listeners three chances to grasp it:

> *'Sales, I'm afraid, are a bit down on the same quarter last year ... By comparison with our successes twelve months ago, these results are disappointing ... This 5% shortfall on the summer revenue target has been rather a setback.'*

OR

> *'I reckon she's the right woman for the job in every way ... She has the qualifications, the contacts, the experience ... Of all the candidates we have considered, this one stands out.'*

In the international arena, people are very happy with this approach. In the mind of the non-native speaker the process goes:

1. 'I know what this is about'   2. 'Ah! Now I get it'   3. 'Good! That's a useful confirmation'.

HOW TO BE CLEAR (7)
PROVIDE A ROUTE MAP & SIGNPOSTS ALONG THE WAY

Sudden surprises can create confusion. In conversation with a foreigner, whose English is limited, you can help comprehension by preparing your listener in advance:

> *'During this meeting we will be talking about four things: the energy consumption of the pump, the costs of maintenance, the stock of spare parts and the amortisation period.'*

Then make it clear when you are changing direction:

> *'I think that covers the energy question. Can we turn now to the maintenance contract?...*
> *So much for maintenance; unless you have any questions, let me point out a couple of worrying things about the spare parts deal...*
> *Well, we've done well on the spare parts question, now let's look at the amortisation...'*

HOW TO BE CLEAR (8)

USE VERIFICATION LOOPS

Say from time to time:

> *'I hope I've been clear so far. Perhaps you could repeat back to me what you've understood. It might save problems later.'*

In a British context this would seem ponderous or pedantic, but anybody working across a language barrier would be happy to double-check comprehension and so avoid expensive embarrassment.

HOW TO BE CLEAR (9)

NAMES? TECHNICALITIES? NUMBERS? JOT THEM DOWN!

How many Frenchmen confuse J with G, I with E?
Should you say 'stroke', 'slash' or 'oblique'?
Can you give your telephone number in the
Italian way? What exactly is the relationship
between a million, a billion and a milliard?
Which languages say 'comma' for the
decimal point? Do you habitually use
the 24-hour clock?

Better safe than sorry: use your PC
screen, office whiteboard or a menu
card to jot it down and share it.

HOW TO BE CLEAR (10)

BE CAREFUL ABOUT TIME

Time is tricky in English: 'I did it', 'I've done it', 'I've been doing it', 'He's coming tomorrow', 'He's going to come tomorrow', 'He'll come tomorrow'. And what about: 'If I hadn't known you'd never done this before, I would have thought you'd been doing it all your life!', and *since, from, to, until, by, yet, just, already, still, ever, always, etc*. We absorb all this in childhood, and often underestimate how hard it is for those who meet English in the schoolroom. So, once again, **double-check arrangements about time**.

HOW TO BE CLEAR (11)

AVOID MULTIPLE NEGATIVES, UNDERSTATEMENT & IRONY

Don't say	Say rather
'I'm not saying it's impossible he'll refuse ...'	*'He might not agree, of course ...'*
'Not a bad drop of wine, that.'	*'Ah! Margaux '64...how marvellous!'*
'Very clever, I must say!'	*'What a silly thing to do!'*

HOW TO BE CLEAR (12)

WATCH OUT FOR FALSE FRIENDS

English is a mongrel language - some Celtic, some Saxon, some Latin. Sometimes, when English has absorbed a word from outside, it has changed its meaning a little.

So what the English see as the 'correct' meaning of the word is out of step with the language it was borrowed from, and also with other languages which have borrowed the same word.

I have just received an e-mail from a German saying 'There will be 20 delegates at the conference, eventually 25'. In German, the word 'eventualisch' means 'possibly' or 'maybe' - just like the French 'eventuellement' or the Italian 'eventualmente'. All are much closer to the original Latin meaning.

The trouble is, I can't be *sure* which way my counterpart is using the word: with German denotation, his message means *'perhaps* an extra five people will turn up', or in the normal English way: 'Five more delegates will arrive later in the week.' I will have to check...

COMMUNICATION ACROSS CULTURES

HOW TO BE CLEAR (13)

COMMON FALSE FRIENDS

Here are the classics. The left column is what you are likely to hear from your counterpart. If his English is less than 100% perfect, the right column is what he might be trying to say.

Global English	Likely meaning
We'll solve the problem eventually.	With a bit of luck, we'll solve the problem.
Actually, it's running at a profit.	Just at the moment, it's running at a profit.
Apparently the figures have been verified.	Obviously the figures have been verified.
This product is definitely not available.	This product will never be available again.
We must control our expenditure.	We must monitor our expenditure.
They have not realised the target.	They have not achieved the target.
Who furnished the transport?	Who supplied the transport?
She invited me to lunch.	She paid for the lunch.
It's a very important benefit.	It's a very large profit.
This is a great hotel.	This is a big hotel.
I don't understand the issue.	I don't understand the result.
What do you mean?	What's your opinion?

66

HOW TO BE CLEAR

EXERCISE

Translate these into global English:

1. Short of taking him out and shooting him, I don't see how we'll ever get shot of him.

2. Far be it from me to quibble over your interpretation of the details, but...

3. You could drive a coach and horses through some of this market research stuff.

4. I'd give an arm and a leg for a shot at that job!

5. They aren't really getting on well, but they'll bloody well just have to get on with it.

(Our version is given on the next page.)

67

HOW TO BE CLEAR

EXERCISE (OUR VERSION)

1. I think it will be difficult to dispose of him.

2. I'm sure you're right about most of the details. However...

3. This market research data is not very convincing.

4. I would really like to do that job!

5. The team isn't very happy together, but they must finish the job somehow.

"Ah! I See."

HOW TO BE CONVINCING (1)

The rules for persuading others have been around for a long time - at least since Aristotle, Cicero and Quintillian set down the rules of rhetoric.

Many readers will have had training in presentation technique, negotiating skills and assertiveness. The effective manager values his communicator's toolkit.

In the following pages, we look at why some of those tools are especially useful when **communicating across cultures.**

HOW TO BE CONVINCING (2)
MAKE A CLEAR STATEMENT OF GOOD INTENTIONS

When we form a positive impression of somebody within our own culture, we base that impression on many unspoken signs - eyes, face, voice, body, tempo, use of language, manners.

Across a culture gap, these signals are distorted. Neither side knows exactly how to interpret the other's unspoken signals. There is interference on the line. So, the only way to establish credibility at the outset is to make a direct statement of it:

> *'Thank you very much for finding the time to meet us today; it means a lot to us. We've been thinking very carefully about the work we all have to do and, of course, we are looking forward to getting to know you and your people better. It's a great opportunity.'*

Even if there are unpleasant facts to face, or difficult decisions to make, it is a good idea to establish a positive momentum from the start.

HOW TO BE CONVINCING (3)
USE THE VISUAL CHANNEL - CAREFULLY

Images are important because they carry ideas straight into the human mind without passing through the machinery of language. Use pictures/diagrams/photographs/ doodles to clarify your meaning and lodge it in the mind of your foreign partner.

At a symbolic level, beware! Is a lion a dangerous animal to be tamed, or the embodiment of national pride? Piggy banks are not used in Muslim countries, where the pig is considered a filthy creature. Not all cultures recognise a tick as YES and a cross as NO. For crucial presentations or campaigns, consult a local specialist and/or an encyclopaedia of symbols.

Be cautious too with metaphors and analogies. When Christ said 'Come with me and I will make you fishers of men', He was *talking to fishermen*. Your verbal images must be familiar to your listener or they will only create anxiety.

Leave out bread and butter *vs* jam, swings *vs* roundabouts, Arsenal *vs* Chelsea, country vicars, Northern landladies and cowboy builders. Find a local equivalent if you can.

HOW TO BE CONVINCING (4)

USE A CLEAR ARGUMENT STRUCTURE

- Mediterranean cultures lean to the inductive argument: 'This is the answer because *a...b...c...*'. **Passionate.**

- Arabic/Asian argument is more circuitous or oblique, avoiding direct statement of the proposal. **Respectful.**

- N.W. European/North American proposals are built on the deductive model: here is the evidence, so we can see that this is the best course of action. **Rational.**

This last is the style that travels best, at least for business purposes. The common ground among decision-makers of all cultures is **evidence and logic**. Try this structure:

1. State the POSITION clearly, including all the information needed to follow your reasoning

2. Outline the PROBLEM - the reason why a decision needs to be made

3. Sketch out the POSSIBILITIES for solving the problem, including all realistic options

4. Eliminating all the less attractive alternatives, state your PROPOSAL clearly and forcefully

HOW TO BE CONVINCING (5)

EMPHASISE EMPATHY & JOINT VISION (WE = YOU + ME)

One of JFK's great lines was 'Ich bin ein Berliner' - claiming personal empathy with the citizens of West Berlin during the Cold War. Aristotle said that logic was only part of the mechanism of persuasion: just as important was to tell your listeners...

- 'I CAN SEE THIS FROM YOUR POINT OF VIEW'

...and to make it clear that

- 'WE'RE WORKING ON THIS TOGETHER'

Show your foreign business partner that you are doing your best to share his or her perceptions. Use a few words of the language (thank you; good morning; cheers!); try to pronounce all names correctly; opt for local specialities in the restaurant; and express curiosity about local history and customs.

If you are an HQ representative visiting a foreign subsidiary, *don't* say '*WE* at HQ think that *YOU* out here should be working harder...'. Instead, say 'If *YOU* and *I* can find a solution, then I'll go back to HQ and tell *THEM* it's all under control.'

73

HOW TO MAKE THE RIGHT IMPRESSION (1)

JOIN THE GLOBAL CULTURE

When I write of showing 'empathy', I don't mean you should change radically your own behaviour. Your Rubovian counterpart knows perfectly well that you are not a Rubovian (just as the real Berliners knew that JFK was not a Berliner). So you only make him uncomfortable if you start aping the Rubovian style. Dick Van Dyke as a Cockney? Peter Sellers as a Frenchman?

BE YOURSELF

There is a middle path: the Global Culture. Suspend the extreme elements of your background culture, and behave so that you are easy and useful as a business partner.

AVOID EXTREMES & BE FLEXIBLE

The Global Culture is seen in the business class lounge of an international airport. Americans are still distinctly American, and Russians come across quite differently, but there is an unspoken agreement about good manners. The language is Global English (see above, *passim*).

HOW TO MAKE THE RIGHT IMPRESSION (2)
LOOK RIGHT & MIND YOUR MANNERS

- **Clothes**: always dress half-a-notch more formally than your counterpart - to show respect.

- **Eyes**: enough eye contact to establish sincerity - but don't come across *too* assertively. Copy the local habit.

- **Manners**: on formal occasions, wait, observe and follow (table manners, particularly). Don't be afraid to ask!

- **Posture, facial expression, voice**: be yourself; you can't go around all day putting on an act.

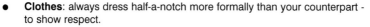

COMMUNICATION ACROSS CULTURES

HOW TO MAKE THE RIGHT IMPRESSION (3)

BE AWARE OF GOOD MANNERS

You will quickly notice many things: the careful way the Japanese exchange business cards; the handshake routine in the French office every morning. These are easy to adapt to, and you should.

Global good manners can be witnessed in hotel lobbies and at the coffee break during international conferences: no rushing, no shouting, no barging in front, no arguments and no swearing. Against this bland background, the Danes appear perhaps a little more brusque, the Spanish more courtly.

Sometimes a foreigner sounds less polite than he intends: instead of 'Could you pass me the sugar?' we hear 'Pass me the sugar'. In many languages politeness depends on using the *vous* or *sie* or *lei* form of the verb; in English English we use circumlocutions like 'I wonder if you would be so kind...'. In Global English these things sound a bit precious and old-fashioned.

One special courtesy: show your foreign partner that you recognise the stress he faces working in a foreign language all day long, by putting frequent breaks in the agenda.

HOW TO MAKE THE RIGHT IMPRESSION (4)

STEADY ON THE 'HUMOUR'

This advice is directed specifically at British readers.

Ask anybody in the developed world what they value about your island culture, and 'sense of humour' will probably come up. Benny Hill, 'Monty Python' and 'Fawlty Towers' made a fantastic impact across N. Europe. Norman Wisdom's old films and TV's 'On the Buses' were very big in the Soviet bloc. Mr. Bean has taken the world by storm. Please notice that this is all rather unsubtle stuff...

Many foreigners* are uncomfortable with that aspect of English humour known as *irony, sarcasm* or *wind-up*. British office life is dominated by 'good-natured' joking. We use dismissive jokes about our products, projects and policies to show that we're not taking things too seriously. If you do the same with your foreign partner, you risk confusing the person or, worse, appearing cynical, insincere or dishonest. So don't.

*One honourable exception: the Finns. They are not a vocal people, but when they do speak it is often to produce a barbed joke aimed at deflating pomposity.

HOW TO MAKE THE RIGHT IMPRESSION (5)

RESPECT THE LOCAL PECKING ORDER

The countries around the North Sea have a 'healthy' attitude to authority. On the HIERARCHICAL << >> DEMOCRATIC axis (page 42) the British, Dutch, Danes, Norwegians or Swedes would get a 5/6. On the MERIT << >> STANDING scale (page 43) they would be at the *merit* end, attaching more importance to a person's energy and achievements than to official status, age, schooling or family origins.

Move east to Germany, or south into France, and the picture begins to change: by Turkey, the scene is definitely HIERARCHICAL, and people take into account each other's STANDING. There is no loss of face if a young Turk defers to his father in front of his friends. Move yet further south and east to Africa and India, and you find tribes with omnipotent chiefs in one, a caste system in the other, and a dedication to professional qualifications and old-boy networks in both. And in the USA, executives feel no shame in changing into a blue suit if Mr Big is on a visit.

Where does the 350 kg gorilla sleep? Exactly where he wants to sleep. Watch your step: don't be too familiar with the big gorilla in front of his subordinates.

COMMUNICATION ACROSS CULTURES

THE INTERNATIONAL TEAM

If you are running a multi-cultural project team, the ideal is simple:

- **Let's get the work done without culture as an issue**

On the other hand:

- **Let's feel free to be curious about each others' cultures**

If this works, it should be possible to resolve cultural problems by talking them through, and make use of cultural tendencies to the team's benefit.

(Who keeps the database in order ... Ingrid? Who runs the brainstorming meeting ... Antonio? Who spurs us on with 'can-do' encouragement ... Hank?)

CODE OF CONDUCT

The final instalment, this time relating specifically to communication:

Code of Cross-cultural Conduct

9. Recognising the extra stress imposed by language barriers, we make allowances for our foreign partner, without appearing patronising.

10. On vital matters, we always double-check understanding, to avoid expensive mistakes.

11. We plan our communication to eliminate the negative and accentuate the positive.

12. Simple, clear, direct, honest and open - the best style for communication across cultures.

COMMUNICATION ACROSS CULTURES

CASE EXAMPLE 5

BACKGROUND

The client company is part of a Korean conglomerate: a manufacturer of electronic goods for home and business markets. They are setting up in Europe through e-commerce, warehouse and high street outlets. An American company is designing a software system to handle the Korean company's distribution.

The project is based in Brussels, with tight quality standards, deadlines and budgets. The team is multinational. Just six weeks in, problems start. Jaime Rodriguez, the Puerto-Rican American project leader, meets his Korean client, who is forthright:

"There is poor communication within your team: sometimes we are asked the same question by two or even three different people. Our time is being wasted because they are badly co-ordinated. One of them blames his colleagues for poor discipline and timekeeping."

Jaime knows it must be Gerhardt Posth. Posth is excellent on technical matters, but he is not liked - a stickler for project management schedules and quality procedures. He always leaves at 1700, even if it means letting a colleague down. (He has never worked outside Germany before.)

COMMUNICATION ACROSS CULTURES

CASE EXAMPLE 5

EXERCISE

Jaime decides to have a talk with Gerhardt. In his imagination, he rehearses the conversation. What might Gerhardt say?

Choose three likely candidates from this list. Think about Jaime's possible responses.

1. Why should I work late simply because other people don't organise themselves correctly?
2. I don't believe in working unpaid overtime.
3. Perhaps we should discuss our work schedules over a beer.
4. Those who arrive late and waste time gossiping and making stupid jokes are bad for team morale.
5. What's the matter with these people: if they've got a complaint why don't they come straight out and tell me?
6. Usually when people talk about *flexibility* they are covering up *laziness* and *inefficiency*.
7. The client is wrong; we work very well together.
8. OK, I'm sorry! I really should learn to relax a bit.

Answer 1, 4 and 6. As for Jaime's response, it could bring into play virtually everything in this book so far.

A HANDFUL OF CULTURES

OUR APPROACH

Remember, it's all relative: the Russians are not *absolutely* sentimental, but they are certainly *more* sentimental than, say, the French Swiss. So the Russians would score a 1 on our EMOTIONAL scale (page 40). Not *all* Americans are completely work-obsessed, but the average American manager (DOING & MEASURING - page 35) definitely works a longer week than, for example, his Norwegian counterpart (BEING & FEELING - page 35). So what is our benchmark?

We are comparing all the *handful of cultures* in this section to N.W. Europe, assuming that most of our readers will be resident there. This does not mean that N.W. Europe is 'correct' and all the others are deviant. Rather, it gives us a reference point: if we say the Chinese are notably LOYAL TO THE TRIBE on our scoring grid (page 33), we are saying that they are more that way inclined than the Germans, Danes or British.

Each cultural cluster is too large and complex for proper treatment in such a confined space. North America: East Coast/West Coast/Small Town? Latin Europe: Madrid/Napoli/the villages of Provence? In every case, the focus is the cultural traits that will affect the way you communicate when doing business.

A HANDFUL OF CULTURES

EXPECTATIONS & BEHAVIOUR

If you are invited to 'drinks at six' in a middle-class English context, you have *expectations*: everybody will be on their feet, drink in hand, and mingling. There will probably be nibbles that you can eat one-handed, but the idea is that you leave before eight and go on somewhere else for your dinner. As for your *behaviour*, there are tacit rules about not getting locked into conversation for too long with any one guest, and avoiding controversial or emotive subjects.

How might your expectations and behaviours be different if the drinks party were in a *dacha* outside Moscow, or on a lakeside restaurant terrace outside Geneva?

For each culture, we hope to give you a few handles: a quick start to building your own model of a given culture. What should I be looking out for? Should I make any adaptations to the way I behave?

N.W. EUROPE

BASIC MODEL

The key here is Hall's pair of polarities (mentioned on page 21):

- MONOCHRONIC *vs* POLYCHRONIC
- LOW CONTEXT *vs* HIGH CONTEXT

N.W. Europe is predominantly 'monochronic, low context'. The people of the region are disciplined in their attitude to time (TIGHT TIME and SINGLE EVENT on our cultural scoresheet); they like to come straight to the point, explain things clearly, get things done (PRAGMATIC, TASK and STATEMENT on the scales). They are uncomfortable with fudged agendas, circular conversations, missing details.

Other values common to the region: DECISIVE not submissive; QUICK RESULTS not big picture; PRIVATE/RESERVED not outgoing/informal; PRESCRIPTIVE not flexible; INHIBITED not emotional. Many people from N.W. Europe believe that this set of values is 'Korrekt' - the only way to do good business.

A HANDFUL OF CULTURES

N.W. EUROPE

GETTING THE MESSAGE ACROSS

There are historical tensions (between the Germans and the Dutch, the Swedes and the Norwegians) but, generally, these are Lutheran, beer-drinking cultures.

Don't
- Flatter your counterpart
- Make promises you might not keep
- Admit that your decisions might be influenced by emotion
- Invade personal body space - hugs, knee-squeezes, etc
- Bend too many rules

Do
- Emphasise quality - especially reliability
- Have complete technical specifications ready
- Stick to the timetable
- Point to measurable benefits within finite timescales
- Stress careful planning over inspired risk-taking

A HANDFUL OF CULTURES

LATIN EUROPE (& SOUTH AMERICA)

From Lutheranism and beer to Catholicism and wine - and olive oil, sunshine, family promenades in the evening: enticing symbols of the Mediterranean. From the scoresheet: LOOSE TIME/MULTIPLE EVENT/THEORETICAL/RELATIONSHIP/SUGGESTION/BIG PICTURE/FLEXIBLE/EMOTIONAL. Our N.W. European business traveller (henceforward NWEuro) should adjust his expectations as follows:

- LOOSE TIME: Business in a leisurely manner. Status goes with mastery of life - of which work is a part only. Seek no reason for this: it is rather the NWEuro who is a freak - a localised product of the protestant work ethic and the Industrial Revolution. Mediterraneans (and Brazilians and Mexicans) live their earthly time as holistic experience. Preparation for Heaven - which is surely not an office block.

- MULTIPLE EVENT: The Latin demonstrates intelligence by his ability to juggle occupations. Your Mediterranean host will sign documents, order coffee, enquire after your health, discuss football/politics/family affairs, and handle the business *all at the same time*.

A HANDFUL OF CULTURES

LATIN EUROPE (& SOUTH AMERICA)

- THEORETICAL: Italian software man talks of Leonardo as the last qualitative scientist; Spanish banker debates macro-economic context; French HR director raises psycho-ethical issues.

- RELATIONSHIP: Time and effort invested in personal bonding - what NWEuros might dismiss as 'small talk'. A good relationship will survive a sticky period of business better than a good deal will survive a bad relationship.

- SUGGESTION: Much is communicated by shrugs, hints and oblique references. If one Mediterranean spells an idea out in elaborate detail, the other might feel slighted: 'This person does not respect my subtlety'.

- BIG PICTURE not quick results. Don't hustle too much.

- FLEXIBLE not prescriptive. 'In Naples a red traffic light is a suggestion'.

- EMOTIONAL not inhibited. Passion, anger, grief ... 'unprofessional' by NWEuro standards.

South American dimensions: Aztec and Inca inheritance down the west side, Indian/Mayan in the hinterland, African/Caribbean on the East, and *yanqui* influence from the North.

CENTRAL & EASTERN EUROPE

For centuries Russians have been debating: 'Are we European or Asian?'. When a NWEuro encounters a Slav, the familiar aspects of his conduct are European (influence from Viking settlers, German engineers, Italian architects, French philosophers, English industrialists), and the most exotic/charming/exasperating are traceable back to the horsemen who swarmed in from the East.

Between Russia and the West stands a tract of cavalry and tank country, agriculturally and industrially rich, with a history of war and shifting national boundaries - Poles, Czechs, Slovaks, Ukrainians, Belorussians.

Moving south and east - through Hungarians, Croats, Macedonians, Albanians, Romanians, Bulgarians - influences from Austria, Turkey, Greece and, even, France become apparent.

Of course, one great event swamped them all: Soviet Bolshevism.

When building your model, be aware of elements in the local background since ancient times, and also of how several generations of central planning and totalitarian bureaucracy have affected people's outlook.

A HANDFUL OF CULTURES

CENTRAL & EASTERN EUROPE

From ancient background

- Image: extended family group 600 years ago in a forest clearing. All slept in the same hut, around the stove. So did guests. Result: open-hearted, soulful, convivial, fond of food, drink, toasts.

- Image: a visitor from the 'advanced' West, scoffing at the Slavs' backwardness, any time in the last 400 years. Result: sensitivity to criticism, guardedness, resignation to poor quality of life, resentment at accidents of birth.

- Image: novels, poems, plays, symphonies, ballets. Result: developed sense of the higher things.

From communist experience

- Propaganda and doublethink   - scepticism about 'corporate values'.
- Authoritarianism and bureaucracy   - lack of confidence in own initiative.
- Shortages and bottlenecks   - make-do-and-mend, pulling strings with cronies.
- Central economic planning   - clumsy negotiation, poor customer service.

A HANDFUL OF CULTURES

THE ARAB WORLD

More broadly expressed: the Islamic world, where that religion is more pervasive in life and business than Christianity in Britain or Buddhism in Japan. Under Islam, there is no separation of Church and State.

Arabs see nothing superior in the western way of life; theirs is a tradition of philosophy, justice, trade, exploration, science, art, literature and cuisine that flourished while N. Europe stagnated in the Dark Ages.

Religion, tradition - and oil wealth, creating super-rich dynasties with geo-political and military tensions all around - (expressed through various brands of Islamic fundamentalism).

The Arab business people you will meet are worldly and sophisticated, and the Koran prescribes tolerance. The NWEuro need not fear rejection, provided he or she observes certain *taboos*.

A HANDFUL OF CULTURES

THE ARAB WORLD

Taboos
- ALCOHOL: tolerance varies country by country, but nowhere should you flaunt it
- DRESS: be modest and respectable
- WOMEN: don't enquire; don't pass comment
- RELIGION: be respectful; don't challenge

Thinking
- The *fatalism* in Moslem culture is often at odds with temporal plans and priorities
- *Traditional* ways are good, perhaps with an overlay of modernity

Working
- Family influence, nepotistic favours, building relationships
- Conversations long, meetings ill-disciplined, agendas non-linear

Communicating
- Lavish praise, forceful rhetoric, educated eloquence
- Close proximity, intimate body language, 'mingling breath'

A HANDFUL OF CULTURES

NORTH AMERICA

USA these days includes African Americans, Hispanics and Native Americans ('Indians') as well as White Middle America. Americans are very conscious of their Irishness, Jewishness, Italianness. Many adult Americans are second- or third-generation immigrants.

It is fun working out which immigrant group imported which cultural habit. For example, the English are struck by how quickly Americans slap you on the back and address you by your most familiar name. This is Irish in origin, surely. As for business culture, Edward Hall was quite clear: corporate America came on the boat from Germany. IBM, Coca-Cola, General Motors - all are *monochronic* and *low context* (see page 21).

Americans are reputedly clumsy in their dealings with non-Americans. Most Americans have no passport. There are two main reasons for cultural insularity:

1. Most white Americans are descended from refugees - political or economic - who had good reason to turn their back on the Old World they ran from.

2. For generations, American business people have had the world's biggest market right on their doorstep: America itself.

NORTH AMERICA

Traditionally there has been a 'special relationship' between America and Britain, although they are 'divided by a common language'.

THE AMERICAN BUSINESS NORM	THE BRITISH BUSINESS NORM
Decisive, quick-minded leadership	Important decisions made over time
Perpetual display of confidence	Diffidence and understatement
Focus on results - especially sales	Focus on relationships and manners
Respect for contracts and deadlines	Respect for the spirit not the letter
Business done over breakfast, lunch, dinner	Lunch for bonding and networking
Steady eye contact, simple language	Intermittent eye contact, oblique word play
New ideas = good ideas	New ideas = provisional ideas
Money as the motivator	Status as the motivator
Jokes = lack of focus	Jokes = sense of proportion

A HANDFUL OF CULTURES

ASIA-PACIFIC

The most enormous of our six huge zones, and the most varied. The cultural groups in the region have been cross-fertilising for centuries - Buddhists with Muslims with Christians, Chinese with Malays with Koreans, British influence with Portuguese with American - while maintaining distinct identities.

They have been in business for 4,000 years, so don't think they have much to learn from a NWEuro. After Rotterdam, the six biggest ports in the world are in this region (Singapore, Kobe, Shanghai, Nagoya, Yokohama, Hong Kong).

What qualities would you want in a manager setting out to break into the fabulous markets of China, or strike a deal with a Japanese consortium? A confident, vigorous, go-getter, perhaps? Hmm...The Asia-Pacific region is characterised by two key cultural principles:

DEFERENCE & HARMONY

ASIA-PACIFIC

The **deferential** aspects stem from the principles of Confucius, 2,500 years ago. He stressed the importance of filial piety and brotherly respect. Unequal relationships, as in the family, bring the stability we all need.

- Subject defers to ruler
- Son defers to father
- Wife defers to husband
- Young defer to old

Asians are aghast at the disorder, delinquency and *loss of face* in the West.

Harmony is achieved through:

- Long discussion before decision
- Moderation, calmness and modesty
- Listening quietly, reacting carefully
- Adherence to ritual and protocol

A HANDFUL OF CULTURES

EXERCISE: PERCEPTION

Who said this?

1. 'I get annoyed when they drift off the agenda. Sometimes hours go by and nothing seems to be decided.'

   a) An Italian about a meeting in Eindhoven?
   b) A Dutchman about a meeting in Bologna?

2. 'He didn't seem very excited by his product - I didn't feel he was really trying to sell it to me.'

   a) A New Yorker about a Londoner?
   b) A Londoner about a New Yorker?

3. 'I found it difficult to get the conversation off the ground; everybody was pretty monosyllabic.'

   a) A Swede about a party in Calcutta?
   b) An Indian about a party in Stockholm?

Answers 1 b, 2 a, 3 b

A HANDFUL OF CULTURES

EXERCISE: BEHAVIOUR

1. A Russian consultant is completing a market research project for your company. He worries that his bank account is not suitable for receiving your payment. Should you:

    a) Give him the e-mail address of your currency transfer specialists?
    b) Offer to pay whatever extra is necessary to open a new account?
    c) Suggest payment in cash?

2. One of your Japanese team is promoted. How should it be announced?

    a) Public announcement; big fanfare.
    b) A series of quiet one-to-one conversations.
    c) A piece of paper on the wall.

3. You are socialising with a Finnish business group. One gets very drunk. You meet him at breakfast. What should you say?

    a) 'The agenda for today's meeting looks very interesting.'
    b) 'Did you enjoy the party?'
    c) 'You were flying last night. How are you this morning?'

Answers: 1 c, 2 b, 3 c

ONE MORE CULTURE: THE EXPATS

Diplomats and soldiers often inhabit a 'home from home' whatever the natives might get up to. The *business* expatriate is compelled to spend that three-year contract in close contact with the local working culture.

Going out
Phase I: Honeymoon. 'Isn't this fascinating! Aren't they hospitable! Such support from home!'
Phase II: Culture shock. 'How can I *live* here! They don't understand! I feel marooned!'
Phase III: Adjustment. 'I used to be so ham-fisted. This can be a fulfilling existence ...'

Coming back
'Everything's changed so much; it doesn't feel like home. We can't maintain our standard of living here on my basic salary, and my partner can't get a job. Must remember not to make disparaging comments about weather/food/service/social life. Why are the children so isolated at school? Maybe we should try for another posting abroad.'

GOOD HABITS

GOOD HABITS

WHAT TO PACK

Passport and tickets, tummy pills - and **a sense of wonder.**

If you are a manager who travels abroad, you are likely to be a confident sort of person - above average, anyway - or you wouldn't get yourself into this. Fine, self-confidence is crucial in strange situations.

Trouble is, self-confidence often leads you to say or think, 'Sure! I can see what's going on here, and I've already started to formulate a plan of action.' In this state of mind, you stifle your curiosity and stop learning.

Swallow your pride; have the courage to admit, 'I'm rather out of my depth here; I'd better ask some questions to find out what's going on.'

Child-like curiosity is a powerful resource.

MAKE FRIENDS WITH THE COOK

My grandfather, Old Bob, advised me in childhood, "When you get moved to a new camp, the most important thing to do is *make friends with the cook*". I never served in the Forces, but I remembered what he said.

When you travel abroad on business, you will be focused on the client, the keynote speaker, the project leader. Fine, but don't forget the driver, the hall porter, the secretary, the interpreter. They can make an enormous difference to your visit, your local reputation, and the reception you enjoy next time round.

In some countries the driver likes you to sit in front beside him; in many the porter appreciates a cheerful greeting and a comment on the weather; in most the secretary likes you to remember her name; in all countries your interpreter thrives on professional respect.

GOOD HABITS

KEEP LEARNING

Read a book...

On pages 21-23 we pay respect to the modern gurus of cross-cultural awareness: Google any of them (eg 'Edward Hall culture book') and you will find their publications. If you want information about a particular country or region, follow the advice on page 20. Or range a bit wider...dig a bit deeper: read a popular novel from your target culture; go back to Marco Polo for the birth of geographical curiosity, Montaigne for the seeds of anthropological 'explanation', or Sir Richard Burton for Victorian derring-do; browse the 'travel' or 'exploration' shelves for Laurens van der Post, Wilfred Thesiger, Lawrence Durrell, Norman Lewis, Paul Theroux, Patrick Leigh Fermor, Eric Newby, Bruce Chatwin...; show off with something about linguistics – Noam Chomsky, anybody?; consider what it all means with one of the popularisers – Alain de Botton, Steven Pinker, Bill Bryson.

...Or take a course

Like the structure of this book, courses, seminars and 'programs' on this subject fall broadly into two categories: the 'generic' – where you raise your awareness and brush up your act for working in situations of 'diversity' – and the 'culture-specific' – which focus on a particular national/racial/tribal group and its habits.

Some are very good, with wise teachers and sensitive training methods; some are uninspired PowerPoint dumps – and if you suspect one of those, stay at home and read a good book instead. If you're in doubt, get in touch with the author.

REMEMBER OUR COMMON HUMANITY

On page 13 the anthropologists get a mention. Theorists of management – Schein and Argyris in particular – have also given us some useful handles on culture, often defined as 'a set of tacit rules' which apply among a given group of people, sometimes to the consternation of people from another group. In either case, the focus is usually on the *differences*, and the advice on training courses (see opposite) is on *how to bridge the culture gap*. Time now for the evolutionary psychologists…

In recent years, a loose group of social scientists have been trying to figure out what lies beneath the differences, to identify 'those features of culture, society, language, behaviour, and psyche for which there are no known exceptions' – features that are 'hard-wired' in our species, placed deep in our brains by the processes of evolution. If we can identify them, then we have the comfort of knowing that wherever we go, we'll observe people doing this stuff, and these insights will enrich the 'models' we build when we travel with our eyes and ears open (see pages 13-20).

'Human universals' are there on the internet. Take a look, and ponder such gems as:
coyness display… nepotism… insults… facial expression of contempt… generosity admired… empathy… planning for future… statuses and roles … reciprocity/revenge… play to perfect skills…

About the Author

John Mattock
John is an independent management consultant and, with his
wife Susanna Lyddon, runs Right Brain Training Ltd,
www.rightbrain.org.uk, from their home in Hampshire.

RBT works the 'soft side' of management training, delivering
in-house courses across all sectors. Events are tailored in
consultation with clients; common themes are presentation
technique, assertiveness, negotiation skills, team building,
cross-cultural sensitivity and conference facilitation.

John has clients from the Baltic to the Mediterranean and from
the Pennines to the Urals, with occasional projects in Asia,
the Middle East and the Americas. He has written several
books: 'The New International Manager', 'Powerful Presentations',
'Russia - the Essential Guide for the Business Traveller' and
'How to be a Better Negotiator' (all Kogan Page).

His satisfaction comes from making poor communicators adequate, and good
communicators great; he has changed many people's working lives for the better.

He dedicates this book to Cecily and Kit, who are teaching him so much.